...And The Soul Remains

Venkatesh E

NOTION PRESS

NOTION PRESS

India. Singapore. Malaysia.

Published by Notion Press 2017

<u>DEDICATION</u>

I wish to dedicate this book to Nature which has remained my inspiration to pen many poems.

I also dedicate this book to all those people who entered my life and stayed in it or left it for various reasons.

This book is also dedicated to those people who have taken time to read many of my poems and have encouraged, motivated or inspired me to write more; as a result of which this book has become a reality today. I am thankful to those people.

CONTENTS

CONTENTS

Foreword

The day I got acquainted with Mr. Venkatesh's poetry, I understood it has something that influences someone.

Poetry, I believe, touches others' lives. He had all the qualities of being an exceptional poet.

This book by Mr. Venkatesh can be considered the greatest work of his career. It is an outstanding work of creativity and skill. Read the wonderful anthology of poems and encourage the budding poet.

Wishing Mr. Venkatesh great success in the new phase of his career.

Dr. Shalini S,
Research Scholar,
Mysuru,
Karnataka.
Date: 13.09.2022

Foreword

Mr. Venkatesh who is a Postgraduate in English Literature, is our college lecturer for English. Teaching is his passion and writing poems has been his hobby for over two decades. He has also written content for websites and voice-over scripts and has done proof reading for doctoral thesis. I wish him all the best in his new venture of publishing the first book with a collection of his poems.

Nagashree H S
Sr. Lecturer
Dept. of Chemistry
Date: 13.09.2022

Preface

This book is a collection of my poems covering various emotions of life. While some are purely imaginary others are true life incidents either I have experienced, or I have witnessed. I have used very simple words so as and when you read the book, the meaning easily enters your brains and touches your heart.

You may share feedback to my email ID evenkatez@gmail.com or WhatsApp me on 9845090764.

Venkatesh E
Lecturer - English
Trainer – CLAT
(Common Law Admission Test)
Teacher – English &
           Social Science (CBSE).
Content Writer
Date: 13.09.2022

1.   THE ALBUM

Those were the time of "black & white"
I was dressed up in colours bright
I was just fourteen years in age
When my first photo was inserted in the first page
That is still a refreshing snap
Even after a long gap

The second page is during my marriage
When I was eighteen years in age
I was nervous and excited
As everyone was invited
That was the day of distress
As I had to smile in stress

The twelfth page in this memories' album
Is the festival moment from
The last celebrated festival of colours
Thrown joyfully over each other
That was still the time of "black & white"
With colours flying high and bright

Come to the thirteenth page
See my children one & two years of age
I enjoyed my childhood with them again
Lot of sacrifices for a small gain
Those are the moments I still miss
When my life was in absolute bliss

Like the petals from a dry flower dropping
My children quit me when they spread their wing
They boarded the flight leaving me alone
They never even called me over the phone
Those who had played on these aged shoulders
Have now chosen the path of their 'late' father

The last photo in this memories' album
Is the prestigious moment from
The capital where I received the award for
My husband's bravery in the border war
That was the time of colours bright
But I was a widow clad in white   ...contd...

The album thus comes to an end
And so will one day her life
That is how a little girl grows
And sacrifices as someone's wife
That is when she becomes a mother
At last left with no one to bother

Those who are in the album today
Will tomorrow be in frames
They will never again come your way
Or even call your names
Love them before they pass away
Before they are buried in the clay
Or set in colourful flames.

2.   DEEP THOUGHTS

Deep thoughts unceasingly haunt my brains
Deep thoughts have left my heart with pains
Deep thoughts of her unwantedly sustains
Deep thoughts are as hard and still like stains
Deep thoughts bring in mind, hot rains

No, I don't want to remember her
For she quit me without my permission
No, I don't want to cry on her
For it was her brave separation

Now I want to forget her
For she kills me day by day
Now I want to hate her
For she loved me but passed away

Yes, I want her to be no where
She seems to me a fiction.
...But I want her to be now here
She is my only satisfaction

She is alive in my thoughts
My heart – A deep ocean
She escaped from this strange ocean
Leaving behind deep thoughts

'She' can be your wife, sister or mother
But she is definitely your need
Do love her when you are together
Because she is a generous tree
And the germinating seed.

3.   TWO FACES OF A COIN

Life is so very easy
It's more beautiful than what you see

Vast green pastureland before our eyes
Solid standing hills covered with ice
The blue ocean with furious strong tide
Cannot believe, world is so big and wide

The sun never fails to rise in the east
To wake up the birds, reptiles, and beast
The seasons never fail to change
Contrasting atmosphere, don't you feel strange?

The trees provide shelter and fruits
Thoroughly useful, be it leaf or roots
The romantic fragrance spread by flowers
Summer, winter, spring and then the rain showers

Hot days replaced by cold nights
The depth of the earth, the hills and heights
Sometimes our friend, sometimes our foe
We are governed by nature from head to toe

The never-ending cyclic forces
The exhaustible natural resources
Climate, calamities, love, hatred, and affection
Life, living, death and ever-growing population

Ever-growing population with majority in poverty
Bonded and bound many, few enjoy liberty
Not been social, they talk about society
Being in the same race, they create enmity

Hard-earned money is spent on habits
The head is not worried what the family eats
His sick wife is lying on the worn-out bed
Let alone medicine, she doesn't find bread

The child watches helplessly, her helpless mother
She is left alone with no one to bother
Moaning with pain, she is ailing on her bed
Unaware that she is on her deathbed   ...contd...

The sun has set; she may not see it again
This may be her last day to suffer in pain
The flowers will no longer provide her fragrance
This day may become her day of 'remembrance'

Take a flower; you'll be pricked by thorns
Beg for mercy, you will never get a chance
Ah!! Life is not so very easy
It's more painful than what you feel and see.

    4.   HIDDEN TRUTH

The gun doesn't care
Who's behind the trigger
Who's before the bullet
Who's wrong, who's correct

The heart knows nothing
In whom it is residing
It has no inkling
Who it is holding

The river doesn't flow
Either fast or slow
Be it a king's command
Or a child's demand

The shadow knows not, the Sun
Decides its direction
If ego blocks the light
The shadow is out of sight

The trees don't stop their shade
Fearing the axe and spade
The leaves betray the trees, once colourful
They degrade to become biofuel

Truth sometimes hinder truthfulness
Lie sometimes create loneliness
Betrayal boomerangs sooner or later
Be it towards a king or a beggar

You aren't rich
If you hold a jumbo sandwich
You will one day plough the sand which
Conceals the earth that you reach
Lifeless and penniless

You aren't rich
If you own something many can't buy
You are definitely rich
If you own something money can't buy.

5.   I WONDER WHY

I wonder why people
Run behind, and not towards success
I wonder why pupil
Run behind marks and not learning process

I wonder why students
Memorise, and not understand lessons
I wonder why parents
Have the habit of comparisons

I wonder why we
Cut the atmosphere-balancing trees
I wonder why he or she
For oxygen and water, say 'please'

I wonder why
The plane, suffers a bird hit
Up in the sky
It's the bird that suffers a plane's hit

I wonder if I am the only one
To wonder about these wonderful errors
I wonder if there is someone
To reflect it like unbiased mirrors.

6.   I WISH I WAS

I wish I was a fountain pen
At your beautiful fingertips
I would have written down all the words
That reside at your lips

I wish I was a wristwatch
Firmly strapped to your wrist
You would have watched me every time
Whenever your wrist you twist

I wish I was a leather wear
That guards your holy feet
I would've protected you from the weather
Wet, dry, cold or heat

I wish I was a pair of clips
That decorate your silky hair
I would have watched you from above
With best and great care

I wish I am in your place
When it is time for you to depart
I would happily let myself go
Forever to stay in your heart.

7.   THEY TOO HAVE HEARTS

Come to the roadside corner any morning
You see a boy dark and thin
He is an orphan and an urchin
Awaiting his meals at the dust bin

Three dogs on the other side waiting their turn
They must feed their puppies in turn
Don't we get something to learn?
How difficult it is, a meal to earn

The dogs are strong and hunt together
The boy is weak and no one to bother
The dogs are called to the doors and fed
The boy hardly succeeds to win a bread

Cute names are given to every dog
The boy is however called a dog
Little kids soothe the dogs with affection
Elders look at the boy with suspicion

There comes a lady with a soiled bag
The bag is cleaner than the boy's rag
All the four animals take position
To welcome the breakfast, it comes as and when

The lady throws the bag from quite a distance
It falls in the bin, tears, and opens
The dogs have struck their luck again
One more attempt of the boy goes in vain

This is not the story of just one day
Such people hardly get a meal per day
It's said every dog must die one day
But such people die every day

Don't ever ignore them and behave rude
They just seek your love and some food.

8.   THE CRY

I still remember the cry
The cry from the eyes gone dry
The cry of an innocent baby's hunger
Signalling his mother with its little finger
To feed it with some food, just little food
Which she was supposed to do, which she should

The little kid was not aware
His father was not someone to care
His father who was drowned in his drink
Had forgotten even the link
Between him and his crying child
How cruel of him, how wild

The kid knew not
The world to which he was brought
Was as cruel as his father
And as helpless as his mother

Those who are uncaring are very rich
Those who care have nothing which
They could have offered this starving kid
And that was what even I did
Had I something to give that day
The innocent child wouldn't have passed away

When the heart falls in love with money
And the drink replaces milk and honey
When thorns of hatred replace flowers of love
When ego lifts people a level above
When earning gives place to lending and borrow
And someone's pleasure leads to someone's sorrow
The pots go empty, and wells go dry
That's when I recall that I
Still remember the pain filled cry.

9.   OF PAINTINGS AND PAINTED THINGS

Ignoring the peace at home
I went on a journey, seeking pleasure
I peeped, I wandered, did nothing but roam
Searching the peak of the tempting treasure

With failure and weakness, when I finally fell
On the cool ocean shore
I spotted an old conch shell
That had been washed ashore

I pressed it against one of my ears
And heard the shell roar and cry
It said a myth dating back to years
The ocean had witnessed with the sky
I was temporarily detached from the world's noise
By the shell's mystical and powerful voice

"Once there was a girl called Clever
Who had two men in her life
One was called Peace and the other Pleasure
Clever was Pleasure's loving wife
While Peace was her friend, calm and clever

Peace knew what and how was Pleasure
But Pleasure always used to suspect
Pleasure was respected by all, under pressure
While Peace always gave and gained respect

Clever always wanted Pleasure by her side
Peace was her need and friend indeed
Peace had a heart broad and wide
Pleasure had in it; hatred buried.

Pleasure's doubt drove him mad
And made him to finally grab
A sharp dagger by which he had
Decided to kill Peace by a stab

Peace, whom he had cunningly befriended
Was now facing the fatal Pleasure
He was attached and he defended
And then gave up to Pleasure's over-power

...contd...

Peace suddenly snatched the dagger of Pleasure
And stabbed it deep into his skin
Peace had stabbed himself with pleasure
And said "I lose, you win,
I did so, not because I am a coward
But only for the sake of Clever
I want her to live like a free bird
And not as a wife to a murderer"

Pleasure in total state of distress
Told Clever how Peace met his end
He had sinned and had to confess
But Clever preferred to die as her friend's friend
Rather than living as a killer's mistress
She drowned herself in the ocean and
Relieved herself from the stress

Pleasure could defeat peace
But could not dominate
Pleasure will be one day forgotten with ease
But Peace is immortal and great"

The conch shell thus ended its story
And showed me the correct road
It showed me the way to peace and glory
And stopped me from riding towards where I rode

I was clever enough to choose peace over pleasure
Choosing pleasure was never the right measure.

10. WINDOW LIFE

From hundred yards away
I see a closed window
A hole in the pane
Movements of a shadow
Hinted a gloomy life in pain
Nothing visible though

Who is at the other side?
A man or woman
Is the house or mind narrow or wide?
No one could guess nor I can
How many alive, how many died
Such thoughts in my mind ran

Whether it's laws of life
Or loss of life
Nothing was clear
From hundred yards near
I could see a closed window
Curiosity raised my eyebrow

And one day the window
Was thrown wide open
No movements to and fro
No idea why and when
The window was left open
Caught my attention

I gathered courage and reached
To look out of the hole in the pane
I could see a beautiful world outside
With nature and ambience enriched
Everyone happy, no one in pain
Everyone's world in their own stride

A life in pain
Looks outside at the beauty
To gain more pain
A life deemed joyous
Sees through the hole
And finds there is chaos

...contd...

Life has multiple elements
Few eliminates life
Few elevates life
If you don't love or live life as a whole
You will end up....behind the window hole.

11. BLESSINGS

Two flowers in my garden
One is a beautiful rose
Blessings from heaven
The other, I won't disclose

While one is fragrant and red
The other is red and fragrant
A blessing in disguise, I say & said
Every time I see, they are vibrant

Two eyes see same image
Two ears hear the same
Two palms together age
But they have a different name

Two feet together cross a stage
To bring wrinkles on our chins
But I gain strength and courage
Every day, with my twins

With both the roses of my garden
Life has become loveable
And has never been ever uneven
Thanks to my daughters, cute and adorable

A mother-daughter relation
Is something beyond description
No poet can do justification
With mere words and expression.

12. DEFINITION

When happiness is not rightly defined
A friend can turn into fiend
A beginning can abruptly end
Things will be difficult to amend
Less you earn, more you spend
Life becomes an unruly blend
When happiness is not rightly defined

When happiness is perfectly defined
It becomes more difficult to find
Heart is restless and so is mind
You forget to be simple & to be kind
Expectations and achievements aren't aligned
All you earn, is left behind
When happiness is perfectly defined

When happiness isn't defined at all
You realise you are happy indeed
Happiness can be in a message or call
Can reside in just a good deed

It need not be searched for
Happiness lies in charity
It isn't complicated & not very far
Happiness lies in simplicity

It need not be always from a smile
Happiness lies in a baby's first cry
Forget your questions for a while
Happiness lies in not asking 'why'

You don't need exorbitant perfume
Happiness lies in first rain's smell
It is derived when you resume
Your forgotten identity, and tell
'Happiness, when isn't defined at all
Is in itself happiness, above all'.

13. WATERFALLS

I saw at places multiple
A variety in you
When in the temple
I saw a deity in you

When in the classes my peer
I saw a lecturer in you
And when with your daughter
I saw a mother in you

While at lunch I saw
A friend in you
And unknowingly this poem
I penned on you

Youngest, but tall are you
I wish you were short
So, if ever we speak
I could bend before you
With respect at peak
From deep down my heart

A spontaneous radiant inspiration
You are the ink of these words
A feeling of inner transformation
When I think of these words

As long as the water
Falls from the waterfalls
You will continue to conquer
Whoever rises, whatever falls.

14. PEEPED

I once peeped into the bedroom
Of a newly wed bride and groom
A child was sleeping by the side
Child's grandparents were beside

I shamelessly peeped into the bedroom
Of a newly wed bride and groom
Shocked, a child was sleeping by the side
With grandparents beside

No jewels adore the bride
No expensive clothes, which was a pride
The groom was dressed in minimum
And all chose to keep mum

No sound but eerie silence
No movements but ambience
No lights but no one in dark
No one to quarrel, none to talk

Why did I once peep into the bedroom?
Of a newlywed bride and groom?
Why was a child sleeping by the side?
With grandparents beside!

Was it their destiny?
Was it their destination?
Was it a curse?
Or was it a course?

Why did I peep into, where I was barred
Why was I amidst buried and charred?
My heart is still jittery and scarred
Why did I visit the graveyard?

15. MIRROR GLASS

Life was happier
When you were my mirror
I saw my beauty
Only I only saw my beauty
I only saw my beauty
I saw only my beauty
I saw only beauty

Life was still happier
When you remained my mirror
I saw how ugly I became
Robbed of my charm and shame
But I could see the beauty in me
Only I could see the beauty in me
I wished they could see the beauty in me

Life became a heap of dried grass
When you turned into transparent glass
There is no transparency around
Noise suppresses musical sound
Beauty conceals ugliness abound
Actors are heroes and celebrities here
Heroes - our soldiers, are left to die there

Money defines rules and regulation
Poverty raises eyebrows and speculation
Failures are leading, leaders are failing
Pots are empty and prisons are filling
Religions have largely barred entry
Caste has become wild card entry
Life is sacrificed for mirror image
I wished you were my mirror in this age
Because when you were my mirror
My life was happier.

16. ABETMENT

A day you will realise, your spouse
Whom you had adamantly chose
Never had and no longer loves
Has deviated from the regular course

Has deviated from the regular course
And is now to someone else close
Has become someone else' source
And had never cared to disclose

Never cared to specify
The reason for deviation
You sit and wonder how to justify
This failed attraction

No ears of your parents to hear
As it was you who chose
Your spouse, during times happier
Standing on the tip of your toes

You feel you are in the dead end
While trying to yourself force
You feel you are dead, and in the end
You apply for divorce

The divorce need not be on papers
It can be a rope and noose
You own all the errors
As it was you to choose

The spouse need not be your husband or wife
Parents need not be father and mother
It can be any decision in your life
For which you were stubborn altogether

Those who are not there
Today on your side
Were once lending their shoulder
For you to reside
Obey them, and their advice you abide
Else your own self will abet you to suicide.

17. CHECKMATE

I was flabbergasted
When you said you hate me
I was devastated
When you said you don't even hate me

To hate someone
It needs a broad heart
To ignore and forget someone
You need to be heartless

The day is not far I guess
When I too will start to hate you
And in this life game chess
My life mate, I will checkmate you

Love is not in love for wealth
Love itself is wealth.

18. MATTERS

It's your presence that matters
Not your proximity
It's your calmness that matters
Not any calamity

It's your visible cheers that matter
Not my concealed tears
It's a minute with you that matters
Not several age or years

It's a great life that matters
Not a long life
It's your life cycle that matters
Not my wrong life.

It's the "you" in you that matter
Not what people around you utter
No one, if not you, matters
If not you, nothing matters.

19. EYES TO ICE

Whether eyes melts with sorrow
Or ice melts with heat
It's water that will flow
Sometimes salty, sometimes sweet

Whether it's painful ears
Or pain filled years
We need to sustain and digest
To emerge the wisest

Whether it's cut-throat words
Or cutting the throat swords
The show must go on
Else our existence and identity are gone

Whether it's your heart, space-less
Or you are heartless
There will be someone to love
Or someone you love, above

Whether your life is less
Or you are lifeless
Whether you have a cue
Or you have no clue
Accept life as it comes to you
Joyfully and without any rue.

20. TO ERR IS HUMAN

The second time I came to this place
I felt I am coming for the first time
All those earlier present had left no trace
They had changed with day and time

It was here I had spent
Fifteen years of my childhood
Those days were fun and pleasant
In a friendly neighbourhood

It was all my mistake
I lacked in sense and wits
When they advised me for my sake
I made issues and conflicts

Now I realise how I was wrong
But am I not too late?
They waited for me years, for long
And finally met their fate

Where do I find them now?
How do I apologise?
To whom shall I express my love?
How do I compromise?

To err is human
But I have committed a sin
There are no chances than I can
Forgive me from within

The places around my eyes
Seem to me like mirrors
They seem to cruelly rise
To point out my errors

My repentance will be my punishment
And it will remain through my age
I happily accept this but also lament
At my own spoilt image

To err is human
To sin is inhuman.

21. DREAM GIRL

Oh! How beautiful is the face of her
No one can come in place of her
Her eyes as beautiful as a fish
She makes me mad and to feel feverish

There she walks like an angel in the sky
I doubt she walks, or can she fly?
She is dressed up in a royal costume
The flowers are jealous to see her bloom

She walks up to me to say hello
I forward towards her dead slow
Her voice is as sweet as nightingale
Crystal clear, soft and pale.

The mild breeze makes her hair to spread
She smiles at me with lips red
She forwards her palm to hold my hand
I felt I am flying between air and land

I felt her touch as soft as feather
Hands in hands we walked together
I was unable to resist her charm
I was excited within and outside calm

She comes for a walk every evening
The sun sets only when she is seen
She makes the moon to wake up and rise
She is an angel, now in human disguise

She is the eighth wonder after the seven
She brings to the earth the joy of heavens
I have never seen someone more beautiful
She makes the atmosphere pleasant and cool

Don't ever set your eyes on her
She is my girl, I love her
You might find it hard to believe
She is a dream I would like to achieve

Unfortunately, she is more heard than seen
She remains to be a girl unseen.

22. FOOD FOR THOUGHT

We sat in a row to have some food
For few grains, I had done all I should
Big plates before, with nothing to eat
Fire was ready, no food to heat

The time we were poverty struck
Fate had brought us bad luck
Hunger made us weak and drove our eyes
To peep greedily for few grains of rice

No difference between thirst and hunger
In either case we just had water
Everything in house were sold for food
Our efforts had brought nothing good

We begged, we snatched, we stole, we cried
"Someone feed us, our pots have dried."
Status, pride, and honesty had no meanings
No time to relax or share our feelings

Our face once always with smiles
Was now dull with smiles away at miles
Days passed by since we counted money
Bread and water replaced fruit and honey

Nobody gave a helping hand
No one wanted us on this land
Found to be unfit on this earth
We weren't eligible even for death

Time is no more the way it was
It was late but had to pass
Today we have a lot to feed
Not just us but for them who need

Poverty made us to learn a lesson
Not for granted anything in possession
What you have today might tomorrow be lost
Today in scarcity might be tomorrow in lots.

23. THE GIFTED PAIN

Oh No! I remembered you once again
To make my wounds feel fresh
The way you hit me on my brain
And threw me inside the sorrow's mesh

Oh No! I remember your soft-soft words
That dragged me towards your heart
The words changed to mightier swords
And tore my heart apart

Oh No! I remember your silent steps
My ears had liked to hear
You still reside in my heart's depths
But I am inside you no where

Oh No! I remember those beautiful moments
That had passed in your presence
They remain as memories of past
Only to be remembered at present

Oh No! I remember your charming face
Which usually wore a happy smile
The smile faded in a slow phase
And never returned, even for a while

Oh No! I remembered you once again
But accept the sorrows and sores
The wounds are but a loveable pain
As they are gift of yours.

24. COUNT UP A COUNT DOWN

One day I saw a man at shore
Two eyes of his could see hopes no more
Three daughters he had, to be married
Four days had passed, he was worried
Five days left for the wedding date to come

Six lakhs cash was the required ransom
Seven people promised but let him down
Eighth wonder was impossible, he decided to drown
Nine steps ahead he stopped to see

Ten minutes in meditation, he enjoyed the sea
Eleven meters ahead a boat he saw
Twelve fishermen fighting the waves' see-saw
Thirteen steps reversed after gaining sense

Fourteen hours after weakness, he displayed confidence
Fifteen minutes later he was back at his house
Fourteen hours he slept and then arose
Thirteen people he met and won the booty

Twelve days of efforts and he did his duty
Eleventh hour sense brought him back
Ten admirers patted him on his back
Nine hours later his daughters were wedded

Eight cars arrived; the party forwarded
Seven seconds are enough to change our fate
Six lakhs were delayed but not too late
Five years might be short, five minutes great

Four shoulders are enough for our journey to end
Three, two or one, one should be a good friend
Two eyes blind is not a handicap
One who sees through mind, adds feather to his cap.

25. SELF POISONING

A decade ago, I wronged to a person
But it wasn't a fact, a mere assumption
Could have been easily solved but did not
During these ten years the matter remained hot
Ego restricted my friend to compromise
Friendship was challenged with rumours and lies
Gone were those days when we walked together
How much ever I tried, results were no better
I lost all hopes of winning him back
Just waited for fate to re-join the track
Keeping in memories those joyful days
Loyally I prayed every day and always
Months and days passed in pain
No news from my friend made me sad again
One day a man knocked at my door
Postman gave a letter with good news in store
Quickly I started, for my friend had invited
Reaching his house, we joyfully united
Sorrow was stuck had for what was done
The day I was released from an undesired burden
United though we were, we were slipping away
Venom of repentance had brought in mind a decay
We could not celebrate and enjoy
Xmas had filled the world with joy
Young but weak and broken, my friend
Zonked with repentance, met his end

New friends always replace the old
But never forget, old is gold
Realise this tomorrow if not today
Before the friend (ship) passes away.

26. MATHEMOTIONS

Sixteen divided by four is four
Your subject is considered to be core
Teaching precision and calculations
You help to negate assumptions

One plus two is three
Your subject will never set you free
Rings, calculus and trigonometry
And then there is geometry

Unit, tens, hundreds and a thousand
The subject will make many a heads bend
There is an algebra, there is arithmetic
That teaches us how to be systematic

Just a position shift
From the right to left
And zero has no value
That's how world is towards you

A negative & positive is still negative
A negative & negative becomes positive
This happens only in mathematics
I wish life had such ethics

Nine minus eight is one
You deal with infinity and ton
Two multiplied by one is two
A variety of problems you are put into

Years and years will pass
In ascertaining the gain and loss
Rules, theorems and formulas
There is no room for flaws

Anything in life is but, not just calculation
Happiness, family, smiles and emotion
Gives you, your heart a better position.

27. ROOT AND ROOT CAUSE

Love becomes the word to be most hated
When it is to someone jokingly stated
Love enters our heart and spreads it venom
The heart becomes the root, our body the stem

Being hated, we ourselves start to hate
We bring ourselves into a depressed state
Our hatred starts to spread its venom
We become the root, the words our stem

We hate the world; we are in turn hated
Our words and deeds are wrongly interpreted
The hatred starts to spread the venom
The world becomes the root
We alone the stem

Life becomes useless when world starts to hate
We bring ourselves into a killing state
We are stung by the venom
Cut off from the root we become a dry stem
Cut off from the root **we become a dry stem**

One track still seems to be intact
It becomes to us a life-giving tract
A stranger's love cleans the venom
The root is again connected to the stem

Being loved, we stop to hate
We bring ourselves to a recovering state
The name is revealed who "love" jokingly stated
She in turn becomes the world's hated
The hatred of the world seems to her a venom
Being the root cause, she becomes the stem.

28. FLASHBACK

Siting sad in a desert, full of sand
Sweating bad in this barren living land
When there was neither charm nor friends around
And to this, my loneliness profound
Had me helplessly surround
I had a dream, I believed to be true
Dark clouds had covered the bright sky blue
The trees started to dance shedding their leaves
Cold breeze brushed through my wet sleeves
Lighting and thunder had created a bashing music
The fresh rain had made the earth fertile
The thick fertile soil gave a pleasant natural smell
How happy I was, how do I tell?
The climate maintained my mood in stride
However, the rain had to one day subside
The sky again appeared bright and blue
It was a dream which I believed to be true

The desert was my life, waste and dry
The sweat was my several attempts and try
The dream was my first love – my college
The dark clouds were my cosmetics of that age
The trees were my friends who made me cheer
Lightning and thunder were ups and downs
Fresh rain was experiences I had to pronounce

Oh! I miss them all today
The dream has just faded away
I remember them all in this sandy desert
The rain has stopped, the sun is set
But there is always a hope of new sun rise
I might come across an exciting surprise
The sky might again become dark and black
Making me fly into my flashback.

29. SOCIAL SATTIRE

Monkeys are imperfect human beings
Human beings are perfect monkeys
They talk more and work the least
They are chameleons and sometimes beast

They eat less and are more drunk
They talk of flying though they are sunk
They replace trees with tall high buildings
They hence spoil their own surroundings

They eat more but grow very less
They curse inside but outside bless
They sacrifice life in the name of God
They become priests though they are fraud

They create enmity, the fight and kill
They invent drugs and themselves fall ill
They run behind money and forget relation
They take all roads but do not reach destination

They make them free by inventing machines
Unaware that these machines drive them to coffins
They fly high to meet a drastic fall
They clear the debris that were once buildings tall

They talk of unity but divide into cast
They ignore future and worry about past
They invent weapons and get killed
They depend on others, being themselves skilled

They talk of society but are not social
They cut those branches on which they dwell
They assault and expose to fulfil their desire
They pull others down to themselves rise higher

One dwell in posh buildings
And one resides on trees
Monkeys are imperfect human beings
Human beings are perfect monkeys.

30. ACCIDENT

And I admitted her flesh and bones
To a nearby hospital
She was still, like the silent stones
Like a flower's withered petal

The final truth was setting upon her
Her life made was setting slowly and slowly
The machine had just passed on her
When her life was settling slowly

Money could not show its power
Prayers also went futile
The fragrant life of the flower
Was escaping every while

The next day....

Beds were in plenty
And so were patients
But her bed was empty
There was an eerie silence

I asked the life-saving doctor
Is she discharged?
That's what I supposed
With a sad smile came the answer
"I am sorry, she is disposed"

The contrasting words made me realise
How inconsistent life is
Her death made me realise
What life is

Life is half spent before we realise what it is
Life is not certain, death certainly is.

31. AFTERMATH

When "is" became "was"
And to her name was prefixed late
It became a concern and a cause
For my present disturbed state

When presence slips into memories
And someone is termed someone's body
Life is no more at ease
It ceases to be thereafter steady

A girl with heart winning looks
Who use to incessantly talk
Alas! Can now be found only in my books
Dumb and silent as a rock

If you ever come across a person
Who is in love with you
Please accept the love without hesitation
And agree you love that person too

For when I stopped a moment to think
She entered into a depression
Red replaced her favorite colour pink
And she died before I could give an explanation

After a month I realised
I too was in love with her
After years I realise
I am in love even now with her.

32. FATAL ATTRACTION

Sitting alone at the seashore one day
I recalled how I used to always enjoy
The sea, the tides, and the wave
With ships appearing like a toy

The sea has secrets of its own
Sometimes crowded with fishermen
Sometimes striking the rock alone
And rocking the shore now and then

The cold breeze during sunset
The sand as soft as cushion
Where will we ever see and get
Such a friendly attraction

My opinions have changed today
For the sea has swallowed my friends
They drowned, they were washed away
They met too sooner their ends

Had I drowned and died
A new life was awaiting upon me
But now that I have survived
My heart is accusing
Had I put that trip aside
My friends would have been here with me

Life is not so easy
It is as mysterious as the sea
The sea has secrets of its own
Sometimes it is crowded by us
Sometimes it makes us alone.

33. SEE OFF

When I had the opportunity to realise
For unknown reasons I closed my eyes
Today I have got to just repent
Recalling the moments with her spent

It all happened because of my "No"
What was in my heart, my lips did not know
Today I am yearning to say "Yes" to her
But she is no more to hear

All my savings could not hold her breath
Moments later they pronounced her death
Only after she breathed her last
I realised we value something when it is lost
I have repented her loss rather being aggrieved
We parted promising to meet beneath the Christmas tree
She departed making me visit her cemetery

When someone takes leave of you
Send them with a smiling see off
As we don't have the smallest clue
It might be our last see off

Think twice before saying to someone "No"
What is in store the next moment, you never know.

34. AN EXAMPLE

A dark old man aged and tired
Who was from life almost retired
Slept in this park some years ago
Until a day he had to finally go

In the remote village school
A boy who was known to be a fool
Learnt the art of making money
And in the business lured many

He played with huge wealth
Unaware of his worsening health
He built a palace with fountains
With desires strong as mountains

His ego made him alone in life
He was deserted by his children and wife
Money made him near to blind
With no one to cry ahead and behind

Loneliness gave freedom and made him an addict
He was drowning in sin bit by bit
He lost everything he gained, with ease
Only to induce the dreaded disease

For some time, he was in the isolation ward
Speaking to others was strictly barred
Fearing the disease may spread, one day
He was thrown out and chased away

A rich young lady threw a coin at him
She walked away never looking at him
The coin made him realise his sin
That brought him from a palace to dustbin
That is when he yearned for life
For the lady who threw a coin at him
Was none other than his beautiful wife

That was the day when in the dark
The old man entered this beautiful park
It is simple to be happy but difficult to be simple
To realise this, the old man is a perfect example.

35. THE BALL IN YOUR COURT

When life was heading towards the end
She came into my life as a helping hand
She was my best and reliable friend
Without her, I knew, I cannot stand

I always held her pressed to my palms
She used to go with me to bed
With her near me, my mind by itself calms
Though I was like a tree with leaves shred

At night I used to feel her beauty
When my fingers ran over her slim body
Though my eyes had poor visibility
She helped me move balanced and steady

And the morning began with her everyday
To the kitchen, to the park
She used to lead me all the way
To and fro, on my walk

When life was in the worst of times
When all my own had deserted me
She came to my aid to replace the rhymes
Bringing the nostalgic medicines of youth in me

...And one day he lost her in the park
Might be to someone of his age
He fell down when he started to walk
Cutting short his own age

His loyal friend would still support
Her newly discovered friend
Though the ball is in a different court
The ball does not have an end

Someone else will very soon pick
This lovely friend known as a
'Walking Stick'.

36. POST MORTEM

When my husband committed suicide
His best friend always sat by his side
He identified my husband's handwriting
And all the while he kept weeping

My husband's sudden demise
Made us to pay a heavy price
We passed through humiliating situations
We begged at the railway stations

It was two years of my husband's death
But still fate was showing us its wreath
The best friend helped us for a while
We were asleep and he escaped meanwhile

One day my husband's enemy happened to see us
He begged for permission to help us
He returned whatever in business he owed
I appreciated him for the gesture he showed
I suspected him as the reason behind the suicide
He proved the actual cause and that he hadn't lied

Soon we shifted to our palatial bungalow
But still we felt something was hollow
The hollow was obviously my husband's absence
Else he would have secured us like a fence

One day someone knocked at our door
A torn cloth was all that he wore
He looked at me and bowed his head
I cared a least but offered him bread

He felt comfortable, I made him eat
Knowing he was a complete cheat
And when he was about to leave
I told him something he could not believe

"You learnt well my husband's signature
But not his character and good nature
You no doubt practiced his bold handwriting
But failed to practice his art of living
You were brave enough to choke him to death   ...contd...

Coward, you did that for his wealth
Had you asked him face to face
We wouldn't have seen those bad days"

He fell on my feet begging
Not to punish him
I knew the best way of punishing
Is not to punish him

A good enemy is better than a bad friend
Punishment pains a while
Not being punished makes us repent till our end.

37. THE WEDDING HALL

When the rumours spread across
In a split second
It resulted in a huge loss
With the wedding coming to an end
The loss was not just monetary
It affected emotions, prestige and pride
Everyone seemed crestfallen with worry
Except the calm and clean bride

The room wore a deserted look
Even the flower withdrew their fragrance
Not even some moments it took
The rumour spread out in an instance

Then there was convincing and crying
Some from the lips, some from the heart
Some were also enjoying
From the bottom of their heart

Among the hues and cries
A confusion was still prevailing
To everyone's shock and surprise
The bride was still smiling

Those who spread the rumour across
Were still walking indoor
They had not calculated the loss
That was yet in store
It was their own idea which was
Responsible for the losses and more

It was midnight and everyone retired
And so did the beautiful bride
But what was done was done
And they will have to repent
They had to break open the doors
To find the bride still and silent
The rumour was cleared with reliable source
But the room was spread with eerie silence

Yes, words are mightier than swords
But silence is stronger than words.

38. ABORTION

You are reading the words of a departed soul
A soul I can bet you cannot console
I thought I was the only prey
I am wrong, I regret to say

I never asked for the life, you gave
I never asked for death and the grave
I accuse each one of you alive there
For not allowing me to live there

Sometimes I kicked, sometimes I curled
I was warm and safe in the safe world
I was happy whenever I slept in the dark
I was shocked I was kept in the dark

I had felt the love in her careful hand
I was sure of all support from behind
Until the day I was shaken with terror
By the hands of the merciless monster

I was ripped and torn apart
The monster detached me part by part
I was dying I realised only then
I wanted to convey my love to her when
I died as my heart was emotionally broken

That was a well-planned clean execution
Of a merciless assassination
I was murdered with cold blooded intention
In the name of an abortion

The tragedy is, you can never hear
My words of love for you my mother.

39. THE FALL

At the age of fifteen
I saw a kid
Who slipped over a banana skin
And fell due to the skid
I laughed at the kid's fall
Along with me, laughed all

At the age of twenty-five
I remembered the kid's innocent fall
I was wondering as to why
The kid cried, why did it fall
Then I got a call
And I forgot it all

At the age of forty-three
I remembered the kid once again
I could not set my mind free
I started to feel its pain
Then I got a call
But the call didn't seem important at all

At the age of eighty
One day I happened to fall
A kid in the vicinity
Smiled at me with its pal
I was left with no helping hand
To help me stand over the slipping sand

Though weak were my eyes
Everything seemed now clear to me
Though huge was my family in size
No one was there near me
The kid came running to me and said
"Shall I help you till your bed?"

The child that fell eighty years ago
Was probably an orphan
I cried within "Oh no
Why did I make fun?"   ...contd...

Whatever you did
How much ever you grow
What you sow is the seed
You have to reap tomorrow
Smile at someone, don't laugh at them
Smile at someone, **don't laugh at them.**

40. CURTAINS DOWN

I know you are there for me
Then why is the delay in arrival
I know you are far from me
But why this interval?

Its time you came to me
And relieved me of my pain
Life is no more the same to me
I feel I am bound to a chain

No life is complete without you
So please come and finish your job
Not everyone happily thinks about you
They just remember you and sob

Please come to me today
And make me immortal
So, people remember me everyday
And speak about me well

For it's a known fact
We are remembered when we're no more
It's a universal truth that
You come to us for sure

When we are happy, when sad
Your entry is a surprise, but I'll be glad
Whether we are good or bad
You come to us, with disguise clad

We all know you, but you are unseen
We remember you only at the end
Your arrival is totally unforeseen
And when you arrive, it's the end.

41. CALAMITY

There a kid is playing with a toy
The parents have let him to completely enjoy
Far away you can hear a mild lullaby
It's already night for a kid, may be

Next to the river some people have gathered today
It's for them, probably a picnic day
A lone farmer is busy on a vast field
It's evident he is working for a bumper yield

Cattles are grazing on the vast meadows
They are grazed upon by black crows
The sound of river flowing in its stride
The beauty of nature is in full pride

Safeguarding the village is a strong mountain
Atop it, is seen a glowing fountain
The people below however do not know
The mountain has in store a volcano

The mountain today in its fullest fury
Has decided to cast a spell of injury
Without a warning it flows downhill
Everyone's victimised by the sudden spill

The village that was, is now an open cemetery
With no people, animals, birds and tree
A boy returns to the village after several years
With a heavy heart, eyes running with tears

He does not know where his home was
He alone knows what is his loss
He stops at a solitary place for a while
Amidst tears there was a short smile

A seed he had long back sown
Has by miracle now grown
Into a lovely shrub with a flower
Hinting the sure possibility for
Growth and population
A miraculous recreation
And a kid might once again play with a toy!!

42. LIMITED LIFE

When life is limited to seven days:
I would go to the silent valleys
Where mind is peaceful, and it sees
The joyful liberty given by nature
Living, non-living things with salient feature

I would walk across the farmers' field
Covered all over by a green shield
That gives us all enough to feed
To survive which is a basic need

I would swim across the lovely river
Which chills and makes me shiver
The river never cares for manmade glories
For it in itself has numerous stories

I would climb the adamant mountains
The origin of falls and fountains
The mountain says, we are here or gone
Life and show must go on

I would go to my ancestral house
The house that never allows
To play a game or music
The house that used to make me sick
Today inspires me to live more and more
Which is not possible, I am sure
The walls are all covered by frames
And one of them is calling my names

I would visit my age-old school
Where every day I used to break a rule
My friends will definitely try to say
They are the fortunate ones today
For their lives are not limited to seven days
How unfortunate they are, my heart says

Finally, I would visit her cemetery
Where her body is captive, and soul set free
I will break open my bodily chains
And in harmony our love
...And the soul remains.